Nuttin' but Pecans

Nuttin' but Pecans

♦

A Collection Of Pecan Recipes

Rosie King

iUniverse, Inc.
New York Lincoln Shanghai

Nuttin' but Pecans
A Collection Of Pecan Recipes

All Rights Reserved © 2004 by Rosemary R. King

No part of this book may be reproduced or transmitted in any form or by any means, graphic, electronic, or mechanical, including photocopying, recording, taping, or by any information storage retrieval system, without the written permission of the publisher.

iUniverse, Inc.

For information address:
iUniverse, Inc.
2021 Pine Lake Road, Suite 100
Lincoln, NE 68512
www.iuniverse.com

ISBN: 0-595-31981-5

Printed in the United States of America

I would like to dedicate this cookbook to the late W. Mavis King, who wished for her recipes to be shared with others. Her collection consisted of many recipes gathered while she and her husband were stationed in various parts of the country by the military, as well as those compiled during their travels to various other countries. I hope you will enjoy a few of her most favorite recipes.

Contents

History of the Pecan 1
What about the Fat? 3
Nutritional Information 5
Measures, Weights, and Substitutions. 7
Soups, Salads, and Vegetables 9
    Pecan Soup 10
    Apple Pecan Stuffed Squash. 11
    Hot Chicken Salad 12
    Summer squash with vinaigrette 13
    Hoppin' John Salad with Toasted Pecans 14
    Fruity Ambrosia. 15
    Pear-Pecan Salad 16
    Pickle Salad 17
    Pecan Couscous Salad 18
    Black Bean, Corn, Pecan and Orzo Salad. 19
    Carrot Salad. 20
    Carrot Pecan Salad. 21
    Spinach Strawberry Salad. 22
    Sweet Potato, Wild Rice and Pecan Salad 23
    Green Bean, Pecan, and Feta Salad 24
    Three Layer Gelatin Mold. 25
    Cranberry Salad. 26
Main Dishes, Meats 27

Penne Pasta with asparagus and pecans..................28
Pecan Chicken Breasts 29
Baked Pecan Oatmeal................................30
Pecan-Coconut Granola..............................31
Bacon Pecan Sandwich Spread........................32
Cajun Pecan Pork...................................33
Brown Rice and Pecan Dressing......................34
Zucchini Bread Pudding 35
Chicken Crunch.....................................36
Pecan-Broccoli Casserole 37
Chicken Salad 38
Pecan Catfish 39
Pecan–Dijon Catfish 40
Southwest Chicken Pecan Quiche 41

Breads, Rolls, Pastries 43

Pumpkin Bread 44
Baked Orange Pecan French Toast....................45
Peppy Pecan Bread..................................46
Honey-Pecan Bread 47
Avocado Pecan Bread................................48
Cranberry Orange Oat Bread.........................49
Sticky Pecan Rolls 50
Zucchini Bread.....................................51

Cakes, Cookies, and Desserts 53

German Sweet Chocolate Cake 54
Maple Pecan Pie....................................55
Pecan Brownies 56
Carrot Cake..57
Apple Nut Dessert 58
Pistachio Cake 59
Southern Style Raisin Pie..........................60
Pecan Cake with Pineapple..........................61

    Green Valley Pecan Pie 62

    Oatmeal Cookies 63

    Nut Butter Ball Cookies 64

    Rum Cake 65

    Impossible Pecan Pie 66

    Texas Cake 67

    Granola Cookies 68

    Cheese Pecan Krispies 69

    Southern Pecan Pie 70

    Chocolate Pecan Bars... 71

    Pecan Crisps 72

    Pecan Cranberry Ice Cream 73

    Hammett House Lemon Pecan Pie 74

    Bananas Foster.. 75

    Pecan Torte 76

    Turtle Cheesecake 77

    Mississippi Mud Cake with Icing.. 79

    Kahlua Pecan Pie.. 80

    Pecan Tarts 81

Candy, Jelly, Preserves 83

    Mexican Fudge 84

    Popcorn Pecan Clusters... 85

    Penuchi 86

    Banana Fudge 87

    Date and Pecan Roll 88

    Microwave Pecan Pralines 89

    Coconut-Pecan Squares... 90

    Pecan Clusters 91

A Word of Thanks

I would like to express my sincere appreciation to all who helped with the production of this special cookbook. To each one who graciously shared your favorite recipes, a special thank you. I would also like to thank the following organizations for allowing me to reprint some of their recipes from their web-sites:

Texas Pecan Growers Association

    (TPGA) College Station, TX

Delta Pecan Orchard, Tutwiler, MS

Glenwood, Inc., Birmingham, AL

North Carolina Pecan Growers Association

    (NCPGA) Raleigh, NC

History of the Pecan

Pecans are part of American history. They are second in popularity, next to peanuts. The United States produces more than eighty percent of the world's pecans, or 324 million pounds a year.

Did you know that the pecan was a native of North America? Well, it is. Fossil remains have been found in Texas and the northern part of Mexico, long before Native Americans inhabited the region. It is felt that this is the original home for the pecan spreading north and east from the area.

The name pecan is an Algonguin American Indian word, paccan or pakan, meaning "all nuts requiring a stone to crack." It was a valued staple food item for Native Americans, and a dominant food resource for some tribes for 2–4 months of the year. Archaeologists have found the dominant concentration of Indian sites in areas where pecan trees were thriving.

The name pecans first appeared in print in 1773. It is also know that George Washington planted pecan trees on his property at Mount Vernon. The trees were a gift from Thomas Jefferson.

Pecan trees can grow to over one hundred feet tall and live to be over a thousand years old. There are over a thousand varieties of pecan trees.

It takes about 10 years for a pecan tree to be ready to produce a viable crop, but that one tree can then produce up to four hundred pounds of nuts in a good year.

The nut grows in clusters of four on the tree. The edible portion of the nut is encased by a very tough outer husk. Upon maturation, the husk splits open to release the pecan. Harvesting is quite a sight! Machine arms hug the base of the tree and shake rhythmically. The nuts are then gathered from the ground. The unshelled nuts are then washed, and polished before selling.

What about the Fat?

It is true that pecans have a high fat content; a pound of pecans packs a whopping 3,633 calories! The pecan has a fat content of nearly 70 percent, the highest of all the nuts. Low carbohydrate enthusiasts will look to this nut to include in their daily plans. OK, that's the down side.

The positive statistics far outweigh the down side. The pecan's fat content is primarily unsaturated, which has been shown to decrease LDL cholesterol levels in the blood. It is also an excellent source of monounsaturated fatty acids, similar to olive oil, which has been shown to be effective in reducing the risk of coronary heart disease. The nut is also rich in vitamin B6, thiamine, zinc, copper, potassium, iron, niacin, selenium, magnesium, phosphorous and vitamin E. The nut is also rich in flavinoids, which act as antioxidants to help reduce the formation of substances in the body that may contribute to cancer and cardiovascular disease. Pecans are a plant food, and thus, are naturally cholesterol-free.

Nutritional Information

One serving size (approximately ¼ cup) shelled pecans will include:

Calories	167
Monounsaturated Fat	10.5 grams
Polyunsaturated Fat	4.2 grams
Saturated Fat	0.25 grams
Cholesterol	0.00 grams
Protein	2 grams
Potassium	98 mg
Phosphorus	73 mg
Calcium	9 mg
Iron	0.5 mg
Zinc	1.4 mg
Vitamin A	32 IU
Vitamin C	0.5 grams
Vitamin E	0.8 mg
Thiamin B1	0.2 mg

Riboflavin B2	0.03 mg
Niacin B3	0.23 mg
Vitamin B6	0.05 mg
Folate	10 mcg
Panotenic	0.43
Dietary Fiber	2 grams
Carbohydrate	4.55 grams

Measures, Weights, and Substitutions

Measurements and Weights

A pinch	1/8 teaspoon or less
3 teaspoons	1 tablespoon
4 tablespoons	1/4 cup
5 1/3 tablespoons	1/3 cup
8 tablespoons	1/2 cup
12 tablespoons	3/4 cup
16 tablespoons	1 cup
2 cups	1 pint
4 cups	1 quart
4 quarts	1 gallon
8 quarts	1 peck
4 pecks	1 bushel
4 ounces	1/4 pound
16 ounces	1 pound
32 ounces	1 quart
8 fluid ounces	1 cup
1 ounce liquid	2 tablespoons

For liquid and dry measurements use standard measuring spoons and cups. All measurements are level.

Substitutions

Ingredient	Quantity	Substitution
Cornstarch	1 ½ teaspoon	1 tablespoon flour
Egg	1	2 egg yolks plus 1 tablespoon water
Fresh whole milk	1 cup	½ cup evaporated milk plus ½ cup water
Unsweetened chocolate	1 ounce	3 tablespoons cocoa plus 1 tablespoon fat
Honey	1 cup	1 ¼ cup sugar plus ¼ cup liquid
Corn syrup	1 cup	1 cup sugar plus ¼ cup water
Tomato sauce	2 cups	¾ cup tomato paste plus 1 cup water
Small onion	1/3 cup chopped	1 teaspoon onion powder or 1 tablespoon dried minced onion
Dry mustard	1 teaspoon	1 tablespoon

Soups, Salads, and Vegetables

Pecan Soup

2 cups **pecan** halves
6 cups beef broth
1 stick butter
2 tablespoons finely chopped green onion
1 clove garlic, pressed
2 tablespoons pureed tomato
1 tablespoon cornstarch dissolved in ¼ cup water
1 egg yolk
½ cup cream
½ teaspoon salt
¼ teaspoon white pepper
1 teaspoon nutmeg

    Grind pecans with broth in blender. Melt butter in a large saucepan, add onions, and cook five minutes over medium heat until soft. Add garlic and cook one minute. Slowly add nut/broth mixture, tomato puree, and cornstarch. Cook for 30 minutes, uncovered, on low heat. Beat egg yolk into cream and slowly whisk into soup; do not boil after this point. Season with salt, pepper and nutmeg.

    (Reprinted with permission from TPGA)

Apple Pecan Stuffed Squash

2 medium acorn squash
2 cups apples, finely chopped
½ cup butter or margarine
1 teaspoon cinnamon
½ teaspoon salt
2 teaspoons lemon juice
1 cup chopped **pecans**
Generous dash nutmeg

Cut squash in half crosswise and remove seeds. Bake, cut side down, in shallow pan at 350° F. for 45 minutes. Remove cooked squash from shells and mix with butter or margarine, apple, cinnamon, salt, lemon juice, and pecans, reserving ¼ cup pecans for topping. Spoon into shells and top with nutmeg and remaining pecans. Bake at 350° F. for 10 minutes. Yield: 4 servings.

(Reprinted with permission from Delta Pecan)

Hot Chicken Salad

2 cups chopped cooked chicken
1 cup chopped celery
½ cup chopped green onions
1 cup mayonnaise
1 tablespoon lemon juice
1 cup chopped **pecans**

Combine all ingredients except pecans and pour into a 1 ½ quart casserole. Top with pecans and bake in a 350° oven for 30 minutes or until thoroughly heated. Yield: 6–8 servings.

(Reprinted with permission from TPGA)

Summer squash with vinaigrette

2 yellow squash, cut into ¼ inch slices
1 medium zucchini, cut into ¼ inch slices
½ small red onion, sliced
3 tablespoons olive oil
3 tablespoons red wine vinegar
½ teaspoon dried basil leaves
Dash of garlic powder
Salt and pepper to taste
¾ cup toasted **pecans**

    Arrange yellow squash and zucchini on a microwave-safe platter. Cover with plastic wrap. Microwave on HIGH (100% power) for 4 minutes. Sprinkle onion over squash; microwave an additional 30 seconds. Combine remaining ingredients; mix well. Spoon over squash. Sprinkle with pecans. Serve hot or chilled. Yield: 4 servings.

    (Reprinted with permission from TPGA)

Hoppin' John Salad with Toasted Pecans

4 cups thawed frozen black-eyed peas or drained canned black-eyed peas
2 teaspoons olive oil, or pecan oil
1 sweet yellow or red onion, finely chopped
1 green bell pepper, seeded and chopped
1 red bell pepper, seeded and chopped
1 fourteen-ounce can of tomatoes, drained and chopped
3 cloves garlic, minced
1 cup long-grain white rice
2 cups defatted reduced-sodium chicken stock
1 teaspoon salt, or to taste
¼ teaspoon cayenne pepper
¾ cup chopped green onions
½ cup chopped toasted **pecans**
Freshly ground black pepper to taste

Drain peas well and set aside. In a large wide saucepan, heat oil over medium heat. Add onions, peppers; stir and cook until softened, about 5 minutes. Add tomatoes and garlic and cook, stirring, for 5 minutes. Add rice and stir for 1 minute to coat the grains. Pour in chicken stock and bring to a simmer. Add salt, cayenne pepper, and reserved black-eyed peas. Cover and simmer on low heat for about 20 minutes, or until liquid has been absorbed. To serve, mound on serving plates and shower with green onions, toasted pecans, and black pepper. Serve hot, warm, or cold. Yield: 6 servings.

(Reprinted with permission from NCPGA)

Fruity Ambrosia

1 pint sour cream
¼ cup confectioners' sugar
2 teaspoons imitation coconut extract
9 cups of apple chunks, sliced bananas, pineapple chunks, and mandarin oranges
1 cup **pecan** halves

Combine sour cream with sugar and extract. Toss with fruit in large bowl. Add pecans. Chill. Yield: (9) 1 cup servings.

(W. Mavis King)

Pear-Pecan Salad

28 ounce can pears
1 cup reserved juice
1 three-ounce package lemon flavored gelatin
1 eight ounce package cream cheese
1 cup chopped **pecans**
½ pint whipping cream

    Drain juice from pears and reserve 1 cup liquid. Bring juice to boil, remove from heat and add gelatin. Chill until partially set. Place pears and cream cheese in blender container and blend until it is a cream consistency. Stir in gelatin mixture. Add pecans. Whip cream and fold into mixture. Pour into 1 large mold or 16 individual molds. Chill and serve on lettuce. Yield: 16 servings.
    (W. Mavis King)

Pickle Salad

1 envelope unflavored gelatin
½ cup cold water
12 cup white vinegar
½ cup water
1 cup water
5 whole cloves
1 can (20 ounces) crushed pineapple, drained
1 cup diced sweet cucumber pickles
½ cup **pecans**

Mix gelatin and cold water; let stand for 5 minutes. Boil vinegar, water, cloves and sugar until it spins a thread. Let cool and remove the whole clove. When cool add the gelatin mixture; pineapple, pickles, and pecans. Chill until firm. Serve on lettuce leaves with mayonnaise.

(W. Mavis King)

Pecan Couscous Salad

1 ½ cups reduced-sodium chicken stock
1 cup couscous (see note)
½ cup chopped toasted **pecans**
1/2 cup parsley
6 tablespoons olive oil
¼ cup freshly squeezed lemon juice
1 tablespoon minced fresh oregano
Salt and freshly ground pepper to taste
2 large tomatoes, peeled, seeded, and chopped (about 2 cups)
4 ounces feta cheese, crumbled

Bring chicken stock to a boil in saucepan. Place couscous in large mixing bowl and stir boiling stock over. Stir and let rest about 15–20 minutes, or until all the stock has been absorbed. Fluff with a fork. Fold in toasted pecans and set aside. Meanwhile, place parsley, oil, lemon juice, oregano, and salt and pepper in a small mixing bowl and whisk together. Add tomatoes and crumbled feta cheese. Pour dressing mixture over couscous, stirring to combine. Taste and adjust seasoning. Chill 30 minutes prior to serving. Yield: 6 servings.

(Note: Couscous is granulated, coarsely ground semolina flour. It is found in the natural foods section of supermarkets.

(Reprinted with permission from NCPGA)

Black Bean, Corn, Pecan and Orzo Salad

8 ounces orzo (rice shaped pasta) or macaroni
¼ teaspoon salt
1 teaspoon olive oil
2 tablespoons freshly squeezed lime juice
3 tablespoons olive oil
¼ teaspoon ground cumin
Freshly ground black pepper to taste
1 cup cooked black beans (canned is fine), drained
1 cup cooked corn kernels
1 small red bell pepper, cored, seeded, and cut into thin slivers
1 ripe tomato, peeled, seeded, and chopped (or 1 cup prepared salsa)
2 green onions, chopped
3 tablespoons chopped fresh cilantro
2 tablespoons chopped fresh parsley
1/3 cup toasted **pecan** halves or chopped **pecans**

Bring a large pot of water to a boil. Add orzo and salt, stir and cook for about 5 minutes, or until orzo or macaroni test done. Drain, toss with teaspoon olive oil and set aside. While pasta is cooking, whisk together lime juice, olive oil, cumin and black pepper. Stir in black beans, corn, orzo, red bell pepper strips, tomato, green onions, cilantro and parsley. Stir in toasted pecans. Taste salad and adjust seasonings. Serve at room temperature or chill 30 minutes prior to serving. Serve on lettuce leaves. Yield: 4 servings.

(Reprinted with permission from NCPGA)

Carrot Salad

1 ½ cup plain yogurt
½ cup mayonnaise
1 teaspoon vanilla
2 pounds grated carrots
½ cup raisons
¼ cup chopped pecans

    Mix yogurt, mayonnaise, and vanilla until blended. Add to carrots, raisons and nuts. Chill. Yield: approx. 8 servings.

    (Rosie King)

Carrot Pecan Salad

1 cup carrots, shredded
1 tablespoon olive oil
2 teaspoons fresh lemon juice
¼ teaspoon salt
¼ cup chopped **pecans**

Toss carrots with oil in bowl. Add remaining ingredients and toss well. Yield: 2 servings.

(Rosie King)

Spinach Strawberry Salad

1 sixteen-ounce bag spinach leaves
2 teaspoons chopped fresh dill or 1 teaspoon drilled dill
3 teaspoons toasted sesame seeds
2 cups fresh strawberries, hulled and sliced in half if large

Dressing

1/3 cup red wine vinegar
¼ cup, plus 2 teaspoon sugar
½ teaspoon onion powder
½ teaspoon garlic powder
¼ teaspoon salt
¾ cup safflower oil
¾ cup chopped **pecans**

Place spinach leaves in large salad bowl. Sprinkle with fresh dill, toasted sesame seeds and strawberries (This can be done up to a couple of hours ahead of serving. Cover with plastic wrap and place in the refrigerator).

Dressing: Combine red wine vinegar and sugar in a medium mixing bowel and whisk until the sugar dissolves. Whisk in onion powder, garlic powder and alt until combined and then whisk in oil. Fold in pecans.

To serve, pour the dressing over the salad and toss to combine. Yield: 8 servings.

(Reprinted with permission from Delta Pecan)

Sweet Potato, Wild Rice and Pecan Salad

2 cups cubed sweet potato (1 inch cubes)
1 tablespoon olive oil
¼ teaspoon salt
1 clove garlic, minced
2/3 cup chopped **pecans**
1 ½ cups uncooked wild rice blend
½ cup shredded carrots
½ cup finely chopped celery
¼ cup dried cranberries or raisins
¼ cup finely chopped red or sweet yellow onion
¼ cup white wine vinegar
2 tablespoons olive oil
1 teaspoon low-sodium soy sauce
1 teaspoon grated orange peel
½ teaspoon coarsely ground black pepper

Preheat oven to 375°. Place sweet potato cubes onto a baking sheet and toss with olive oil, salt and garlic. Roast 30–35 minutes, turning once with a spatula, or until potatoes are cooked through and begin to brown. Remove from oven then set aside (this can be done a day ahead). Place pecans in a foil pie pan and place in oven still warm from the potatoes. Turn off heat and let pecans toast in turned off oven about 15 minutes, until they turn golden brown and smell fragrant. Remove from oven to cool. Cook rice according to package directions, omitting salt and fat. Set aside to cool. In a large mixing bowl, combine sweet potatoes, pecans, rice, carrots, celery, cranberries and onion. Stir to mix well. Sprinkle vinegar, olive oil, soy sauce, orange peel and black pepper over salad mixture and stir so that salad absorbs dressing. Serve at once, or chill and serve later. Yield: 8 servings.

(Reprinted with permission from NCPGA)

Green Bean, Pecan, and Feta Salad

2 pounds fresh green beans, trimmed
1 small purple onion, thinly sliced
1 (4 ounce) package crumbled feta cheese
1 ¼ cup chopped **pecans**, toasted
¾ cup olive oil
¼ cup red wine vinegar
1 tablespoon chopped fresh dill
½ teaspoon minced garlic
Salt and pepper to taste

    Cut green beans into thirds, and arrange in a steamer basket over boiling water. Cover and steam 15 minutes or until crisp and tender. Immediately place in colander and run cold water over the beans to stop the cooking process; drain and pat dry. Toss together olive oil, vinegar, dill, garlic, salt and pepper; cover and chill for 1 hour. Pour vinaigrette over green bean mixture, and chill 1 hour; toss just before serving. Yield: 8 servings

    (Rosie King)

Three Layer Gelatin Mold

1 three-ounce package strawberry gelatin
3 ½ cups boiling water
1 sixteen-ounce can whole cranberry sauce
1 three-ounce package lemon gelatin
1 eight-ounce package cream cheese
1 nine-ounce can crushed pineapple, undrained
½ cup chopped **pecans**
1 three-ounce package lime gelatin
2 tablespoons sugar
1 sixteen-ounce can grapefruit sections

Dissolve strawberry gelatin in 1 ¼ cups boiling water; add cranberry sauce, mixing well. Chill until partially set. Pour into 8-cup ring mold. Chill until almost firm. Dissolve lemon gelatin in 1 ¼ cups boiling water; add cream cheese. Beat until smooth with rotary beater. Add pineapple; chill until partially set. Stir in pecans; ladle gently over cranberry layer in mold. Chill until almost firm. Dissolve lime gelatin in remaining boiling water (1 cup); add sugar and stir to dissolve. Add undrained grapefruit. Chill until partially set; pour gently over cheese layer. Chill overnight. Unmold. Yield: 10–12 servings.

(W. Mavis King)

Cranberry Salad

1 envelope unflavored gelatin
1 ¼ cups cold water
1 cup sugar
½ cup chopped celery
½ cup chopped **pecans**
½ teaspoon salt
2 cups cranberries–fresh

    Cook cranberries in 1 cup water for 20 minutes. Stir in sugar and cook another 5 minutes. Set aside. Place gelatin in 1/3 cup cold water and dissolve. Add to hot cranberries. Stir until dissolved. Cool. This will thicken slightly. Add celery, pecans, and salt. Place in mold that has been washed in cold water. Refrigerate for at least 2–3 hours. This recipe may be doubled.
    (Carolyn Sutherland)

Main Dishes, Meats

Penne Pasta with asparagus and pecans

1 tablespoon olive oil
1 tablespoon butter
1 lb. asparagus, cut into 2" pieces
1 yellow bell pepper, diced
1 red bell pepper, diced
1 teaspoon minced garlic
1 ¾ cups chicken broth
1 lb. penne pasta, uncooked
1 ½ tablespoons minced fresh basil
2/3 cup Parmesan cheese, divided
¾ cup toasted **pecans**, divided
Salt, pepper to taste

    Combine olive oil and butter in a large skillet; add asparagus and cook until lightly browned, stirring constantly, about 6–7 minutes. Stir in peppers and garlic and cook about 1 minute. Add chicken broth, bring to a boil. Reduce heat and add pasta and basil. Simmer 7–9 minutes. Stir in half the Parmesan cheese and half the pecans. Add salt and pepper to taste. To serve, transfer to a warm bowl and sprinkle with the remaining cheese and pecans. Yield: 4–6 servings.

    (Reprinted with permission from TPGA)

Pecan Chicken Breasts

4 boneless, skinless chicken breasts
1 cup flour
1 teaspoon salt
½ teaspoon freshly ground black pepper
2 egg whites, beaten until frothy
6 tablespoons creole mustard, divided
1 cup finely ground **pecans**
1 cup fresh bread crumbs
¼ cup vegetable oil
½ cup skimmed evaporated milk
Toasted **pecans**

Combine flour, salt, and pepper in a shallow bowl. Blend egg whites and 4 tablespoons mustard in a second bowl. Combine pecans and breadcrumbs in a third bowl. Dredge each chicken breast in flour, shaking off excess, then in egg white mixture, then in pecan mixture. Press so that coating adheres to both sides. Heat oil in a large skillet over medium high heat. Cook chicken breasts about 3 minutes or until crisp and brown. Turn, reduce heat to medium and cook about 5 minutes or until chicken has lost its pinkness. Meanwhile, in a 1 quart saucepan, warm evaporated milk over medium heat. Stir in remaining mustard. Cook about 5 minutes or until heated. To serve, slice chicken breasts diagonally and top with sauce. Sprinkle with toasted pecan halves. Yield: 4 servings.

(Reprinted with permission from Delta Pecan)

Baked Pecan Oatmeal

½ cup canola oil
1 cup brown sugar
2 eggs
1 cup chopped **pecans**
3 cups quick oatmeal (uncooked)
1 tablespoon baking powder
1 cup skim milk
Nutmeg, cinnamon to taste

Combine oil, sugar, eggs, and pecans in a large bowl. Mix well. Add oatmeal, baking powder and milk. Pour into a light greased 9x13 pan. Sprinkle lightly with nutmeg and cinnamon. Bake 350° F. for 30 minutes. Cut into squares, serve hot or cold, with milk or fruit. Yield: 8–10 servings.

(Reprinted with permission from Delta Pecan)

Pecan-Coconut Granola

¾ cup firmly packed light brown sugar
½ cup canola oil
½ cup water
¼ cup butter or margarine
½ cup chopped **pecans**
½ cup sweetened flaked coconut
1 teaspoon ground cinnamon
1 ½ cups uncooked oats
1/3 cup raisons or chopped dates

    Cook first 4 ingredients over medium heat in a large saucepan, stirring constantly, until butter melts. Stir in pecans, coconut and cinnamon. Add oats; toss well to coat. Spread in a light greased 15x10 inch pan. Bake at 350° F. for 35 minutes or until golden brown, stirring occasionally. Remove from oven. Stir in raisins, cool completely. Enjoy it with milk as a cereal or sprinkle over yogurt or fresh fruit, or really splurge and sprinkle over homemade vanilla ice cream.

    Reprinted with permission from Delta Pecan)

Bacon Pecan Sandwich Spread

6 slices bacon
1 cup chopped **pecans**, toasted
1 cup grated sharp Cheddar cheese
1 teaspoon grated onion
½ cup mayonnaise
½ teaspoon salt

Cook bacon until crisp; drain and crumble. Combine with other ingredients. Refrigerate at least 1 hour to blend flavors. Spread on pumpernickel bread. Yield: about 2 ½ cups.

(Reprinted with permission from TPGA)

Cajun Pecan Pork

¾ cup **pecan** halves, toasted
¾ cup fine, dry breadcrumbs
¼ teaspoon salt
½ teaspoon paprika
¼ teaspoon dried oregano
¼ teaspoon ground red pepper
6 (4 ounce) lean boneless pork loin chops
¼ cup whole wheat flour
½ cup buttermilk
Vegetable cooking spray

Process first 6 ingredients in a blender until pecans are finely chopped. Dredge pork chops in flour. Dip in buttermilk; dredge in pecan mixture. Chill 1 hour. Arrange pork on a rack coated with cooking spray. Place rack in a 13x9 inch pan. Coat pork evenly with cooking spray. Bake at 425° s for 15 minutes. Turn port, and coat evenly with cooking spray. Bake 5 more minutes or until done.

(Rosie King)

Brown Rice and Pecan Dressing

2 cups uncooked brown rice
5 cups chicken broth
1 teaspoon salt
2 cups chopped onions
2 cups chopped celery
2 cloves garlic, minced
¼ teaspoon black pepper
½ teaspoon poultry seasoning
1 cup chopped **pecans**

    Combine rice, chicken broth and salt. Heat to boiling, stirring once. Reduce heat and simmer, covered for 45 minutes. Cook onions, celery and garlic until tender in a pan that has been lightly sprayed with non-stick coating. Stir in cooked rice. Add pepper, poultry seasoning and pecans. Serve with roasted turkey or baked chicken. Yield: 12 (½ cup) servings.

    (Reprinted with permission from TPGA)

Zucchini Bread Pudding

2 medium zucchini, sliced ¼ inch thick
½ cup frozen whole kernel corn
2 tablespoons olive oil
½ cup chopped roasted red sweet peppers
1 tablespoon each minced fresh garlic, snipped fresh basil, snipped fresh parsley, and snipped fresh sage
5 cups 1 inch sourdough or Italian bread cubes
4 oz. Swiss cheese shredded
3 tablespoons chopped toasted **pecans**
2 cups half-and-half or light cream
5 eggs, slightly beaten
1 teaspoon salt
¼ teaspoon pepper

    Preheat oven to 350° F. Grease a 2 quart rectangular or oval baking dish; set aside. In a large skillet cook zucchini and corn in hot oil for 3 minutes. Stir in sweet peppers, garlic, basil, parsley, and sage. Cook and stir for 2 minutes more or until zucchini is tender. Stir in bread. Place half of the mixture in prepared dish. Sprinkle with half of the cheese. Repeat layers. Sprinkle with nuts. In a medium bowl whisk together half-and-half, eggs, salt, and pepper. Carefully pour over bread mixture. Bake uncovered for 35 minutes, or until a knife inserted near the center come out clean. Yield: 6 servings.

    (Reprinted with permission from Delta Pecan)

Chicken Crunch

10 ounces cream of mushroom soup
½ cup milk
1 teaspoon parsley flakes
8 boneless chicken breasts
1 package stuffing mix
2 tablespoons butter, melted
½ cup toasted **pecans**

Mix soup, milk, parsley flakes and onion. Dip chicken breasts in soup mixture, and then roll in stuffing mix and pecans. Shape like a potato; put in a baking dish. Pour butter over. Bake at 350° F. for 1 hour. Cover with foil to prevent browning too quickly. Yield: 8 servings.

(Reprinted with permission from Delta Pecan)

Pecan-Broccoli Casserole

1 twenty-ounce packages frozen chopped broccoli
1 10 ¾ ounce can condensed cream of mushroom soup
½ cup mayonnaise
1 cup chopped **pecans**
1 large onion, finely chopped
2 eggs, well beaten
1 cup grated sharp cheese
2 cups bread crumbs

Cook broccoli according to package directions. Drain. Add soup, mayonnaise and pecans. Mix well. Add onion and eggs. Pour into greased 2 quart casserole dish. Sprinkle with grated cheese and top with bread crumbs. Bake at 350° F. for 30 minutes. Yield: 6–8 servings.

(Rosie King)

Chicken Salad

2 teaspoons mayonnaise
2 teaspoons plain yogurt
1/8 teaspoon curry powder
1 cooked chicken breast, cut into ½ inch pieces
1 stalk celery, coarsely chopped
3 lettuce leaves, washed and dried
2 mushrooms, thinly sliced
4 slices cucumber
2 sugar snap peas
3 **pecan** halves

In a small bowl, stir together mayonnaise, yogurt, and curry powder. Fold in chicken, celery, and grapes. Line a plate of lettuce leaves, mushrooms, cucumber, broccoli, and snap peas, top with chicken salad and garnish with pecan halves. Yield: 1 serving

(Rosie King)

Pecan Catfish

2 farm raised catfish fillets
1 teaspoon salt
1 teaspoon pepper
1 cup finely chopped **pecans**
½ cup cornmeal
½ cup butter or margarine
½ cup whipping cream
2 tablespoons lemon juice
1 tablespoon chopped fresh parsley

Garnishes:

Lemon wedges, chopped parsley, and chopped pecans

Sprinkle fish with ½ teaspoon salt and pepper. Stir together ½ cup pecans and cornmeal–dredge fish in mixture; melt ¼ cup butter in 3 quart sauté pan over medium-high heat; add fish and cook 7 minutes on each side or until fish flakes easily with fork. Remove from skillet. Melt remaining ¼ cup butter in pan over medium-high heat. Add remaining ½ cup pecans; cook, stirring constantly, 1 minute. Add whipping cream, lemon juice, remaining salt and pepper; cook 1 minute. Remove from h eat; stir in parsley. Serve over fish. Garnish as desired. Yield: 4 servings.

(Reprinted with permission from Delta Pecan)

Pecan–Dijon Catfish

2 catfish fillets
Salt and pepper to taste
¼ cup Dijon mustard
¼ cup melted butter
½ cup dry bread crumbs
¾ cup chopped **pecans**
Nonstick cooking spray

Preheat oven to 475° F. Rinse fillets, pat dry and place, rounded side up, on a greased baking sheet. Season to taste with salt and pepper. Brush each fillet with 1–1 ½ tablespoons mustard. Combine butter, bread crumbs and pecans. Spread ¼ of the pecan-crumb mixture over each fillet, pressing firmly. Spray each fillet with nonstick cooking spray. Bake each fillet with nonstick cooking spray. Bake for 13–15 minutes, or until fish flakes easily when tested with a fork and the top surface in a golden brown. Yield: 4 servings.

(Rosie King)

Southwest Chicken Pecan Quiche

1 pie shell 9 inches, baked
1 cup cooked chicken, finely chopped
1 cup grated Swiss cheese
1/3 cup Mexican style Cheddar Jack–finely shredded cheese
1/3 cup chopped onion
1 tablespoon flour
½ cup chopped **pecans**
2 eggs, beaten
1 cup milk
½ teaspoon Dijon mustard
3 tablespoons medium or hot salsa

Mix chicken, cheeses, onion, flour, and pecans. Sprinkle into cooled crust. Mix, eggs, milk, mustard, and salsa. Pour over chicken. Bake in 325° oven for 50 minutes. Yield: 4 servings.

(Rosie King)

Breads, Rolls, Pastries

Pumpkin Bread

1 cup water
1 cup vegetable oil
2 cups cooked, mashed pumpkin
3 cups sugar
3 eggs
1 cup chopped **pecans**
1 ½ cup chopped dates
3 ½ cups self rising flour
2 teaspoons baking soda
2 teaspoons ground cinnamon
1 teaspoon ground nutmeg
1 teaspoon ground ginger
1 teaspoon ground cloves
1 teaspoon salt
½ teaspoon baking powder

Combine water, oil, pumpkin, sugar, eggs, pecans, and dates in a large mixing bowl; mix well. Combine flour, baking soda, cinnamon, nutmeg, ginger, cloves, salt and baking powder. Add to pumpkin mixture and blend thoroughly. Pour into 2 greased 9x5x3 inch loaf pans. Bake in a 350° oven for 1 ½ hours. Yield: 2 loaves.

(Reprinted with permission from TPGA)

Baked Orange Pecan French Toast

4 eggs
2/3 cup orange juice
1/3 cup milk
¼ cup sugar
½ teaspoon vanilla
¼ teaspoon ground nutmeg
8 one half-inch thick slices Italian or French bread or Texas toast
¼ cup butter or margarine
½ cup chopped **pecans**

Beat together eggs, juice, milk, sugar, vanilla, and nutmeg. Arrange bread in a single layer, top with egg mixture. Refrigerate at least 2 hours. Melt butter in 10x15x 2 pan, and arrange bread on top. Bake at 350° F. for 20 minutes. Sprinkle with pecans and bake 10 minutes more.

(Reprinted with permission from Delta pecan)

Peppy Pecan Bread

½ cup warm water
2 packages dry yeast
1 ¾ cup lukewarm milk
3 tablespoons sugar
2 tablespoons shortening
1 tablespoon salt
7 ½ cups flour
1 bell pepper, diced
½ cup pimento
½ cup chopped onion
2 cups grated cheese
¾ cup chopped **pecans**

Dissolve 2 packages yeast in ½ cup warm water. Mix milk, sugar, salt and shortening well. Add yeast. Add half the flour and mix well. Add the remaining flour a little at a time, mixing well after each addition. Add peppers, pimento, onions, cheese and pecans. Work in only enough flour to make handling easy. Knead until smooth. Place in a clean greased bowl. Let rise until double in bulk. Knead again for about 5 minutes. Divide dough into two equal parts. Shape into a loaf. Place in well-greased loaf pan. Bake at 350° F. for about 20–25 minutes, until nicely brown. Remove from oven and grease loaves with margarine. Delicious with barbecued meats or any kind of sandwiches.

(Jo Ann Zinsmeyer, Castroville, Texas–TPGA).

Honey-Pecan Bread

Nonstick cooking spray
¼ cup margarine
1 cup honey
1 ¼ cups whole wheat flour
1 ¼ cups all-purpose flour
2 teaspoons baking powder
1 teaspoon baking soda
¼ teaspoon salt
1 large eggs plus 2 egg whites, lightly beaten
½ cup chopped **pecans**

Preheat oven to 325° F. Spray two 7 1/2x2x3 ½ inch loaf pans lightly with non-stick spray. Heat margarine and honey in small saucepan over medium heat until margarine is melted. Combine whole wheat flour, all-purpose flour, baking powder, baking soda and salt in large bowl. Add margarine mixture and beaten eggs and stir until well blended. Fold in pecans. Pour into prepared pans. Bake 40–45 minut4es, until toothpick inserted in center of loaf comes out moist but not wet. Cool on wire rack 10 minutes. Invert onto wire rack; remove loaves from pans and cool completely. Yield: 2 loaves with 10 servings each.

(W. Mavis King)

Avocado Pecan Bread

2 cups all-purpose flour
¾ cup sugar
1 teaspoon baking soda
½ teaspoon baking powder
¼ teaspoon salt
1 egg, slightly beaten
½ cup buttermilk
1 cup mashed soft avocado
1 teaspoon lemon juice
½ cup **pecans**, coarsely chopped

    Measure flour, sugar, soda, baking powder and salt into large mixing bowl. Stir to combine. Add egg, buttermilk, avocado and lemon juice. Mix until thoroughly combined. Stir in pecans. Pour into well-greased 9x5x3 inch loaf pan. Bake in 350° oven 60–65 minutes or until wooden pick inserted in center comes out clean. Cool 10 minutes. Remove from pan. Yield: 16 slices.
    (W. Mavis King).

Cranberry Orange Oat Bread

1 ¾ cups all-purpose flour
1 tablespoon baking powder
¼ teaspoon salt
2 eggs
2/3 cup milk
2/3 cup sugar
1 tablespoon grated orange ring
1/3 cup orange juice
¼ cup oil
1 ½ cups oat flakes
1 cup chopped cranberries
¾ cup chopped **pecans**

Mix flour with baking powder and salt. Beat eggs, milk, sugar, orange ring, orange juice and oil; add to flour mixture and mix just enough to moisten flour. Stir in cereal, cranberries and nuts. Pour into well-greased 9x5 inch loaf pan. Bake at 350° F. for 60 minutes or until tester inserted in center comes out clean. Cook in pan 10 minutes. Remove from pan and finish cooling on rack. Yield: 18 (1/2 inch) slices.

(Rosie King)

Sticky Pecan Rolls

¼ teaspoon baking soda
¼ cup granulated sugar
1 teaspoon salt
1 package active dry yeast
2 ½ cups flour, unsifted
1 cup buttermilk
3 tablespoons canola oil
2 tablespoons water
¼ cup melted butter or margarine
½ cup firmly packed brown sugar
¾ cup **pecan** halves
1 teaspoon ground cinnamon

In a mixer bowl, combine soda, granulated sugar, salt, yeast, and 1 cup of the flour. Heat buttermilk and oil to very warm (120–130°), add to flour mixture, and beat at medium speed for 2 minutes. Stir in 1 ½ cups flour; knead until smooth and elastic, adding more flour as needed. Combine water, 2 tablespoons of the butter, and ¼ cup of the brown sugar; distribute in 12 muffin cups; top mixture with pecans. Roll dough to a 12x15 inch rectangle. Brush with remaining butter; top with remaining brown sugar and cinnamon. Roll into a cylinder, cut in 12 slices, and place in muffin cups. Let rise in a warm place until doubled, or 1 ½ hours. Bake in a 350° F. oven until golden, about 20–25 minutes. Yield: 12 rolls.

(W. Mavis King)

Zucchini Bread

3 eggs
1 cup oil
1 cup sugar
1 cup brown sugar
2 cups grated zucchini
3 teaspoons vanilla
4 teaspoons baking powder
1 teaspoon salt
1 teaspoons cinnamon
½ cup chopped **pecans**

    Beat eggs until light, mix next 4 ingredients. Sift dry ingredients; add pecans, mix well. Place in 2 well greased and floured loaf pans. Bake at 325° for 70 minutes.

    Cool. Yield: 2 loaves bread.

    (Rosie King)

Cakes, Cookies, and Desserts

German Sweet Chocolate Cake

4 ounce bar of Baker's German Sweet Chocolate
1 cup margarine
½ cup boiling water
4 egg yolks
2 cups sugar
2 ½ cups cake flour
1 teaspoon vanilla
½ teaspoon salt
1 teaspoon baking soda
4 egg whites, stiffly beaten

Melt chocolate over boiling water. Cool. Cream margarine and sugar until fluffy. Add yolks, one at a time, beating well after each. Blend in vanilla and chocolate. Sift flour, soda, and salt; add alternately with buttermilk to chocolate mixture, beating after each addition until smooth. Fold in beaten egg whites. Pour into 3 greased and floured 8" layer cake pans. Bake at 350° F. for 30–34 minutes. Cool.

Coconut-Pecan Frosting

1 1/3 cups evaporated milk
1 1/3 cups sugar
3 slightly beaten egg yolks
¾ cup margarine
1 teaspoon vanilla
2 cups coconut
1 cup chopped **pecans**

Combine all ingredients; cook and stir over medium heat until thick, about 12 minutes. Add the coconut and pecans. Cool until thick enough to spread. Garnish with pecans on top.

(Reprinted with permission from NCPGA)

Maple Pecan Pie

4 eggs
1 ½ cup Maple syrup
Pinch of salt
1 teaspoon vanilla
5 tablespoons butter, melted
1 ½ cups of **pecans**
1 nine-inch unbaked pie crust

    Preheat oven to 400° F. Beat eggs with syrup. Add salt, vanilla and butter. Spread pecans on the pie crust. Pour on the egg mixture. Bake for 10 minutes at 400° F. Lower heat to 300° F and bake for 35 minutes. Yield: 6 servings.

    (Reprinted with permission from Delta Pecan)

Pecan Brownies

2/3 cup margarine
4 squares Bakers unsweetened chocolate
2 cups sugar
4 eggs
1 ½ cups flour
1 teaspoon baking powder
½ teaspoon salt
1 cup chopped **pecans**
2 teaspoons vanilla

Melt margarine and chocolate over boiling water. Cool. In another bowl, add sugar gradually to well beaten eggs. Add chocolate mixture and blend. Add flour, baking powder and salt; mix well. Add pecans and vanilla. Mix well. Bake in greased and floured 13x9x2 pan in 350° F. oven for 30 minutes. Cool in pan. Yield: 16 brownies.

(Janet Paulk)

Carrot Cake

2 cups flour
2 cups sugar
2 teaspoons baking soda
2 teaspoons cinnamon
1 teaspoon salt
4 eggs, beaten
1 1/3 cup oil
3 cups raw carrots, finely grated
½ cup chopped **pecans**

Sift dry ingredients. Add eggs and oil. Stir and add grated carrots and pecans. Bake at 350° F. in lightly greased and floured Bundt pan for 55 minutes.

Icing:

½ box powdered sugar
4 ounces cream cheese
½ stick margarine
½ teaspoon vanilla
½ cup chopped **pecans**

Blend all ingredients; spread on cooled cake.
(Gloria Gust)

Apple Nut Dessert

1 cup sugar
¾ cup sifted, all purpose flour
2 teaspoons baking powder
1 tablespoon soft shortening
½ cup evaporated milk
1 teaspoon vanilla
½ cup chopped **pecans**
3 cups cut up peeled apples

Topping

2 tablespoons brown sugar
1/3 cup flour
2 tablespoons softened butter or margarine

Mix with fork in a 2 quart mixing bowl, sugar, flour, baking powder and soft shortening. Stir in evaporated milk and vanilla until well mixed. Stir in pecans and apples until coated with batter. Spread in greased 9-inch square pan. In another bowl, mix with fork until crumbly brown sugar, flour, and margarine or butter. Sprinkle over apple mixture. Bake in 400° F. oven for 30–35 minutes, or until top is golden brown. Serve warm or cold. Spoon into dishes or cut into 9 squares. If desired, top with ice cream. Yield: 9 servings.

(W. Mavis King)

Pistachio Cake

¼ cup sugar
3/4 cup finely chopped **pecans**
1 teaspoon cinnamon
1 package yellow cake mix, with pudding included
1 package (4 serving size) Pistachio Flavor Instant Pudding and Pie filling
4 eggs
½ cup sour cream
¼ cup oil
½ teaspoon almond extract
10 drops green food coloring

    Combine sugar, pecans, and cinnamon; set aside. Combine remaining ingredients in large mixing bowl. Blend; then beat at medium speed with electric mixer for 4 minutes. Pour one third of the batter into greased and floured 10 inch fluted tube or tube pan; sprinkle with half the sugar mixture. Repeat layers and top with remaining batter. Bake at 350° for 45–50 minutes or until cake tester inserted in center comes out clean. Cool in pan for 15 minutes. Remove and finish cooling on rack. Yield: 12 slices.
    (Rosie King)

Southern Style Raisin Pie

1 cup sugar
2 beaten eggs
6 tablespoons butter
¼ cup milk
1 cup raisins
½ cup chopped **pecans**
1 eight-inch unbaked pie shell

Gradually add sugar to the eggs. Add the butter and milk. Stir in raisins and pecans. Pour into the pie shell. Bake in a 350° F. oven for 40–45 minutes. Cool. Serve with whipped cream. Yield: 6 servings.

(W. Mavis King)

Pecan Cake with Pineapple

1 ½ cups sugar
2 cups flour
2 teaspoons baking soda
½ teaspoon salt
3 eggs
2 teaspoons vanilla
¼ cup applesauce
1 twenty-ounce can crushed pineapple
½ cup chopped **pecans**

    Mix ingredients for cake and bake in greased and floured 9x13x2-inch pan at 350° F. for 35 minutes, or until done. Frost with cream cheese frosting.

Cream cheese frosting

8 ounces softened cream cheese
1 tablespoon softened butter
2 cups powdered sugar
2 teaspoons vanilla
1 cup chopped **pecans**

    Combine all ingredients and frost on cooled cake.
(Rosie King)

Green Valley Pecan Pie

1 cup light corn syrup
1 cup sugar
2 eggs
1 cup whipping cream
2 tablespoons butter
2 tablespoons yellow cornmeal
2 tablespoons all-purpose flour
½ teaspoon vanilla
2 ½ cups chopped **pecans**
1 nine-inch pie crust–unbaked
1 small orange
¼ cup ½ pecans

    Beat together until well blended the corn syrup, sugar, eggs, 2 tablespoons of the whipping cream, butter, cornmeal, flour and vanilla. Stir in the pecans and pour into the pastry shell. Place remaining ½ pecans on top of pie. Bake pie on a rack in the lower third of a 350° oven until center is et when pan is gently shaken, 40–45 minutes. Let cool at least 30 minutes; serve warm or cool. Whip remaining whipping cream until it holds soft peaks; sweeten to taste with sugar. Pare orange colored part of peel from the orange and cut into very thin slivers. Offer whipped cream and slivered orange peel to top individual wedges of pie. Yield: 6 slices.
    (Rosie King)

Oatmeal Cookies

1 cup shortening
1 cup brown sugar
1 cup white sugar
2 eggs
1 teaspoon vanilla
3 cups oatmeal
1 ¾ cup flour
½ teaspoon salt
1 teaspoon baking soda
½ cup chopped **pecans**
½ cup coconut

Cream shortening with sugar. Add beaten eggs, vanilla, and oatmeal. Sift flour, baking soda, salt; add pecans and coconut. Mix well. Make into small balls, flatten somewhat and bake at 375° F. for 10–12 minutes.

(W. Mavis King)

Nut Butter Ball Cookies

1 cup soft butter or margarine
½ cup sugar–confectioners
½ teaspoon salt
2 teaspoon vanilla
2 cups sifted flour
1–2 cups finely chopped **pecans**

Mix butter with sugar until creamy. Add the rest of the ingredients; mix well. Refrigerate until easy to handle–approximately 1 hour. Using fingers, shape into balls. Place onto ungreased cookie sheet. Bake 10–12 minutes. DO NOT BROWN. Roll balls into powdered sugar. Yield: approx. 4 dozen.

(Rosie King)

Rum Cake

1 cup chopped **pecans**
1 package yellow cake mix
1 (3 ¾ ounce) package vanilla pudding mix
4 eggs
½ cup cold water
½ cup oil
½ cup rum

Sprinkle nuts over bottom of 12-cup Bundt pan. Mix all cake ingredients together. Pour batter over nuts. Bake in 325° oven for 1 hour. Cool for at least 15 minutes. Invert on serving plate. Prick top of cake with fork.

Glaze

¼ pound butter
¼ cup water
1 cup granulated sugar
½ cup rum

Melt butter in saucepan. Stir in water and sugar. Boil 5 minutes, stirring constantly. Remove from heat. Stir in rum.

Drizzle and smooth glaze evenly over top and sides. Allow cake to absorb glaze. Repeat until glaze is used up.

Yield: 12 slices.

(Rosie King)

Impossible Pecan Pie

4 eggs, beaten well
1 ¾ cups sugar
½ cup flour
½ cup margarine
½ cup coconut
½ cup chopped **pecans**

    Mix the sugar and flour together then add to the well-beaten eggs. Melt the margarine and add to the egg mixture. Fold in the nuts and coconut. Mix together and pour into a well-greased pit pan. Bake at 350° F. for 35–40 minutes.

    (David Przestrzelski)

Texas Cake

1 cup oil
2 cups sugar
3 eggs
1 jar apricot strained baby food
1 jar blueberry buckle baby food
½ teaspoon cinnamon
½ teaspoon nutmeg
1 teaspoon soda
½ teaspoon salt
2 cups flour
1 teaspoon vanilla
1 cup chopped **pecans**

Cream together oil, sugar and eggs (added one at a time). Add remaining ingredients one at a time, stirring until well mixed. Bake in a 12-cup-Bundt pan at 350° for 1 hour or until done. Yield: 12 slices.

(Florence Freeland)

Granola Cookies

½ cup salad oil
1/3 cup molasses
¼ cup water
2 eggs
1 ¼ cups sugar
2 cups flour
1 teaspoon soda
1 teaspoon salt
1 teaspoon cinnamon
1 tablespoon nonfat dried milk
2 cups granola
1 cup raisons
½ cup chopped **pecans**

Heat oven to 375° F. Mix oil, molasses, water, eggs, and sugar thoroughly. Stir in remaining ingredients. Drop dough by rounded teaspoonfuls 2 inches apart onto lightly greased baking sheet. Bake 8–10 minutes or until almost no imprint remains when touched with finger. Cool slightly before removing from baking sheet. Yield: 7 dozen.

(W. Mavis King)

Cheese Pecan Krispies

16 ounces shredded cheese, medium sharp
1 stick butter or margarine
2 cups plain flour
2 cups Rice Krispies Cereal
Pecan halves
Red pepper to taste
Lawry's Seasoning salt or Accent

    Allow cheese and butter to reach room temperature. Cream together adding red pepper to taste. Add flour and mix. Stir in Rice Krispies by hand and mix. At this point you will want to take small pieces of dough and make into a ball similar to making cookies. If dough is hard to handle you may wish to chill before handling. Place ball on cookie sheet and flatten with a fork. Top with pecan halves and sprinkle with Lawry's seasoning and store in an airtight container. Yield: 8 dozen.

    (Reprinted with permission from Glenwood, Inc.)

Southern Pecan Pie

1 nine-inch unbaked pie shell, deep dish
3 eggs
1/8 teaspoon salt
½ cup sugar
1 tablespoon plain flour
1 cup clear or white Karo syrup (see note)
¼ cup melted butter
1 cup **pecans** (chopped, or halves)

    Beat eggs and salt. Mix in flour and sugar. Gradually add syrup, beat well. Add melted butter and pecans. Pour into pie shell. Bake in a 350° oven for 45–60 minutes. Pie is done when pie cracks.

    (Note: Syrup choice can vary by your personal tastes. Using a thick clear syrup gives you a mild sweet pie. Using a more traditional darker syrup will add more distinct maple flavor and a syrup in between even another distinct variety. The choice is your so experiment to see which one you like best. For best results use only thick syrup. Yield: 6 slices.

    (Reprinted with permission from Glenwood, Inc.)

Chocolate Pecan Bars

1/14 cups unsifted flour
1 cup confectioners' sugar
1/3 cup unsweetened cocoa
1 cup cold margarine or butter
1 (14-ounce) can Eagle Brand Sweetened condensed milk (Not evaporated milk)
1 egg
2 teaspoons vanilla extract
1 cup chopped **pecans**

    Preheat oven to 350° F. (325° F. for glass dish). In large bowl, combine flour, sugar, and cocoa; cut in margarine until crumbly. Press firmly on bottom of 13x9–inch baking pan. Bake 15 minutes. Meanwhile, in medium bowl, combine sweetened condensed mile, egg and vanilla; mix well. Stir in nuts. Spread evenly over crust. Bake 25 minutes or until lightly browned. Cool. Cut into bars. Store covered in refrigerator. Yield: 24–36 bars.

    (Reprinted with permission from TPGA)

Pecan Crisps

½ cup shortening
½ cup butter or margarine
2 ½ cups brown sugar
2 well beaten eggs
2 ½ cups sifted flour
½ teaspoon soda
½ teaspoon salt
1 cup chopped **pecans**

Cream shortening, butter, sugars, and eggs. Sift dry ingredients. Add pecans. Drop from spoon onto lightly greased cookie sheet. Bake in 350° F. oven for 12–15 minutes.

(W. Mavis King)

Pecan Cranberry Ice Cream

1 cup toasted **pecan** pieces
1 cup (14 ounces) sweetened condensed milk
¼ cup lemon juice
1 twenty-ounce can crushed pineapple
1 sixteen-ounce can whole berry cranberry sauce
1 sixteen-ounce carton whipped cream

In a bowl combine milk and lemon juice, pineapple, cranberries and pecans. Fold in whipped cream. Spoon into a 13x9 inch pan. Freeze until firm. Cut into squares. Yield: 12–16 squares.

(Reprinted with permission from TPGA)

Hammett House Lemon Pecan Pie

3 whole eggs
1/3 stick margarine (do not use whipped)
1 ½ cups white sugar
¾ cup **pecan** halves or pieces
1 teaspoon lemon extract
Juice of ½ lemon (2–3 tablespoons)

Mix ingredients in order given, but do not use a mixer or beat until frothy. Pour into 8" unbaked pie shell. Put in preheated oven 350° F. and bake about 10 minutes, then cut the oven temperature to 300° F. and bake until crust is browned and pie filling is set. Too rapid cooking will cause pecans to scorch and crust to brown before center of pie has finished cooking. For variety, try Orange Pecan Pie substituting juice of ½ fresh orange for the lemon juice and 1 teaspoon orange extract in lieu of lemon extract.

Yield: 6 servings.

(Ginny Hoffer)

Bananas Foster

Pint vanilla ice cream
4 large bananas
¼ cup banana liqueur (you can substitute ¼ cup water
½ cup dark rum
6 tablespoons rum
¼ cup packed light brown sugar
½ teaspoon ground cinnamon
1 cup chopped **pecan** pieces

Cover a small-rimmed baking sheet with parchment paper and place in the freezer for 10 minutes. When chilled, remove pan from freezer. Quickly scoop ice cream into 12 small balls, and place on chilled parchment-lined sheet. Keep in freezer until firm and ready to serve, at least 1 hour and up to 1 day ahead.

When ready to serve, peel bananas and quarter them, cutting lengthwise and then crosswise; set aside. Pour banana liqueur and dark rum into separate glass measuring cups; set aside. Heat 3 tablespoons butter in a large skillet over medium heat. Sprinkle sugar and cinnamon over butter, and cook until sugar is dissolved. Remove pan from heat, and carefully stir in banana liqueur. Add bananas, flat side down and cook until softened and lightly browned on the bottom. Remove pan from heat and add rum. Return to heat, and cook about 10 seconds to allow rum to heat up. If using a gas stove, carefully tip the pan away from you until the vapors from the rum ignite (Alternatively, light the rum with a long match. When the flames have subsided, remove pan from heat and gently stir in remaining 3 tablespoons butter. Place 3 scoops of ice cream in each of 4 bowls. Spoon the banana mixture and the sauce over each. Sprinkle with pecan pieces and serve immediately. Yield: 4 servings.

(Reprinted with permission from Delta Pecan)

Pecan Torte

5 egg whites
1 1/3 cups graham cracker crumbs
1 cup sugar
1 1/3 teaspoon baking powder
1 1/3 teaspoon vanilla
1 cup coarsely chopped **pecans**

Beat eggs until stiff; gradually add sugar and baking powder. Fold in crumbs, pecans and vanilla. Pour into 9-inch pie pan. Bake at 350° F. for 25–30 minutes or until puffed and golden. Yield: 6 servings.

(Ginny Hoffer)

Turtle Cheesecake

Crust:

1 cup vanilla wafer crumbs
¼ cup chopped **pecans**
2 tablespoons brown sugar
½ cup melted butter

Filling:

3 (8 oz) packages cream cheese
3 large eggs, slightly beaten
1 (8 oz.) package sour cream
1 cup granulated sugar
2 teaspoons vanilla

Topping:

1 cup dark brown sugar
¼ cup unsalted butter
2 tablespoons whipping cream
¼ cup chopped **pecans**
¼ cup mini chocolate chips
1 cup halved **pecans**

Mix crust ingredients in bowl until crumbs are moistened. Press mixture over bottom of lightly buttered 9-inch springform pan. Refrigerate to chill. Heat oven to 375° F. Put filling ingredients into large mixing bowl. Beat until well blended. Pour over chilled crust. Bake until edges are set, about 1 hour. Do not over bake. Remove cake from oven; cool on rack. Cover lightly with plastic wrap. Chill several hours. Put brown sugar, butter and cream into medium saucepan. Heat to a boil over high heat; stir until sugar is dissolved. Cool slightly; pour over cake. Sprinkle top of the center of cake with nuts and chocolate chips.

Arrange pecan halves at the rim of the cake in a circle. Yield: 12 slices of cheesecake.

(Reprinted with permission from Delta Pecan)

Mississippi Mud Cake with Icing

Cake:

2 stick butter
4 eggs
1 teaspoon vanilla
1/3 cup cocoa
2 cups sugar
1 ½ cups flour
1 cup chopped **pecans**
1 package miniature marshmallows

Icing:

1 box powdered sugar, sifted
1/3 cup milk
1 teaspoon milk
1 teaspoon vanilla
1/3 cup cocoa
1 stick softened butter

Grease a 9x11 pan. Cream butter, add eggs and vanilla. Sift cocoa, sugar, flour and salt and add to creamed mixture. Mix well and add nuts. This will be a thick mixture and you have to spread it into the pan. Bake at 350° F. for about 45 minutes. Remove cake from oven and place one whole package of miniature marshmallows on top of cake and put back into oven until brown.

Icing: Combine powdered sugar, milk, vanilla, cocoa, and butter and mix well. When cake is cool, put icing on top. Yield: 16–24 squares.

(Reprinted with permission from Delta Pecan)

Kahlua Pecan Pie

¾ cup sugar
¼ cup butter, softened
1 teaspoon vanilla
3 eggs
½ cup plus 1 teaspoon Kahlua
½ cup dark corn syrup
¾ cup evaporated milk
1 cup whole or chopped **pecans**
1 unbaked 9 inch pastry shell, chilled
½ cup whipping cream, whipped
Pecan halves

In mixing bowl, combine sugar, butter, vanilla and flour, mixing well. Add eggs, beating well after each addition. Stir in Kahlua, syrup, evaporated milk and 1 cup pecans, mixing thoroughly. Spread batter in chilled pastry shell. Bake at 400 F. for 10 minutes, then reduce oven temperature to 325° F and bake an additional 40 minutes or until firm. Chill pie. Just before serving, garnish with whipped cream and pecan halves. Yield: 6–8 servings.

(Reprinted with permission from Delta Pecan)

Pecan Tarts

Crust:

1 cup butter
1 cup sugar
4 egg yolks
2 teaspoons almond extract
4 cups sifted

Filling:

1 cup butter
2/3 cup Karo Dark Corn Syrup
2 cups confectioners sugar
2 cups chopped **pecans**

To make crust: Mix butter and sugar, stir in egg yolks, almond extract and flour. Press into small muffin cups, then bake at 400° 8–10 minutes.

To make filling: Bring to a boil the butter, corn syrup and confectioners sugar, and then stir in the pecans. Spoon into the shells and bake at 350° for 5 minutes. Yield: 4 dozen

(Nancy Swinford).

Candy, Jelly, Preserves

Mexican Fudge

2 cups sugar
½ cup evaporated milk
1 cup pecans
½ cup margarine
½ cup white corn syrup
1 teaspoon vanilla

Cook sugar, evaporated milk, pecans, margarine and corn syrup in saucepan over medium heat until mixture reaches soft, ball stage. Add vanilla. Beat until cool and creamy. Drop by teaspoon on wax paper.

(Reprinted with permission from TPGA)

Popcorn Pecan Clusters

1 ½ quarts popped popcorn
1/cup **pecans**
½ cup butter
1 cup brown sugar
¼ cup honey
½ teaspoon salt
¼ teaspoon cinnamon
¼ teaspoon nutmeg
1 tablespoon water

    Combine popcorn and pecans. Keep warm in a 250° oven. In a two-quart saucepan, melt butter. Stir in brown sugar, honey, salt, cinnamon, nutmeg and water. Cook over medium heat until boiling, stirring constantly. Boil mixture to hard crack stage (250° F. on candy thermometer). Place the popcorn mixture in a large bowl. Slowly pour honey glaze over popcorn mixture, stirring to coat. Spread in a buttered jelly roll pan, and return to a 250° F. oven for 20 minutes, stirring once after about 10 minutes. Break into pieces. Yield: 2 ½ quarts.
    (Rosie King)

Penuchi

2 cups brown sugar
2/3 cup thin cream
1 tablespoon butter
1 teaspoon vanilla
1 cup chopped **pecans**

Combine sugar and milk in a saucepan and, stirring constantly to prevent scorching, cook to 236°, or until it forms a soft ball when tested in cold water. Remove from heat; add butter and allow it to cool to 110°. Beat until creamy; add vanilla and pecans and stir. Pour out onto a slightly buttered pan or platter.

(W. Mavis King)

Banana Fudge

2/3 cup milk
2/tablespoons light corn syrup
2 cups sugar
2 ripe bananas, mashed
2 tablespoons butter
½ teaspoon vanilla
1 cup chopped **pecans**

   Combine milk, corn syrup and sugar in a saucepan and stir until sugar is dissolved. Add mashed bananas and blend. Cook over moderate heat, stirring occasionally, until a small amount of liquid dropped into cold water forms a soft ball (235° on candy thermometer). Remove from heat and stir in butter, vanilla, and pecan. Set saucepan in pan of cool water to cool. Then beat until smooth. Pour into a lightly buttered dish and cut into squared when firm.

   (W. Mavis King)

Date and Pecan Roll

2 cups sugar
¾ cup evaporated milk
½ pound dates
1 cup chopped **pecans**
1 tablespoon butter

    Mix sugar, milk and dates in a saucepan. Heat, stirring constantly, until it comes to a boil. Cook to 240° (use a candy thermometer). Remove from heat and add the pecans and butter. Cool, and then beat mixture until creamy. Pour out onto a damp cloth. Shape into a long roll 1 1/2 inches in diameter. Chill until firm enough to slice.

    (W. Mavis King)

Microwave Pecan Pralines

One box brown sugar
½ pint of heavy whipping cream
2 tablespoons of butter
2 cups of **pecan** halves
1 teaspoon of vanilla

Microwave brown sugar and whipping cream for 13 minutes on HIGH in a 5-quart container.

Add butter, pecans, and vanilla. Mix well and drop by spoonfuls onto aluminum foil. Let cool and start eating!

(Reprinted with permission from TPGA-Barbara Galland)

Coconut-Pecan Squares

½ cup butter
½ cup dark brown sugar
1 cup flour
2 eggs
1 cup light brown sugar
1 cup coarsely chopped pecans
½ cup shredded coconut
2 tablespoons flour
1 teaspoon vanilla
Pinch salt
Confectioner's sugar

Cream butter with dark brown sugar; add flour and mix well. Press into a greased 8x8x2 square pan, spreading batter evenly into the corners. Meanwhile, beat eggs until frothy. Gradually add light brown sugar and shredded coconut, which has been tossed with flour. Season with vanilla and pinch of salt. Mix well. Spread over baked crust. Bake for 20 minutes more or until well browned. Sprinkle with confectioner's sugar when cool and cut into 1-inch squares. Yield: 64 squares.
(W. Mavis King)

Pecan Clusters

½ cup sugar
½ cup evaporated milk
1 tablespoon corn syrup
1 cup semi-sweet chocolate morsels
1 cup chopped **pecans**

    Put into a heavy 2-quart saucepan sugar, evaporated milk, and corn syrup. Stir over medium heat until mixture boils and is bubbly all over top. Boil and stir over medium heat 2 minutes more. Remove from heat. Stir in chocolate morsels until completely melted. Stir in pecan. Drop with 2 teaspoons on wax paper. Chill until set. Yield: 24 clusters.
    (W. Mavis King)

0-595-31981-5

Printed in the United States
68570LVS00010B/217